Shard

by Julie Murray

Dash!
LEVELED READERS
An Imprint of Abdo Zoom • abdopublishing.com

3

3 Dash!
LEVELED READERS

Level 1 – Beginning
Short and simple sentences with familiar words or patterns for children who are beginning to understand how letters and sounds go together.

Level 2 – Emerging
Longer words and sentences with more complex language patterns for readers who are practicing common words and letter sounds.

Level 3 – Transitional
More developed language and vocabulary for readers who are becoming more independent.

abdopublishing.com

Published by Abdo Zoom, a division of ABDO, PO Box 398166, Minneapolis, Minnesota 55439.
Copyright © 2019 by Abdo Consulting Group, Inc. International copyrights reserved in all countries.
No part of this book may be reproduced in any form without written permission from the publisher.
Dash!™ is a trademark and logo of Abdo Zoom.

Printed in the United States of America, North Mankato, Minnesota.
052018
092018

Photo Credits: Alamy, AP Images, iStock, Shutterstock
Production Contributors: Kenny Abdo, Jennie Forsberg, Grace Hansen, John Hansen
Design Contributors: Dorothy Toth, Neil Klinepier

Library of Congress Control Number: 2017960596

Publisher's Cataloging in Publication Data

Names: Murray, Julie, author.
Title: The Shard / by Julie Murray.
Description: Minneapolis, Minnesota : Abdo Zoom, 2019. | Series: Super structures |
    Includes online resources and index.
Identifiers: ISBN 9781532123139 (lib.bdg.) | ISBN 9781532124112 (ebook) |
    ISBN 9781532124600 (Read-to-me ebook)
Subjects: LCSH: Shard, The (London, England)--Juvenile literature. | London (England)--Buildings,
    structures, etc--Juvenile literature. | Architecture--building design--Juvenile literature. | Structural
    design--Juvenile literature.
Classification: DDC 720.48309--dc23

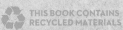

Table of Contents

The Shard

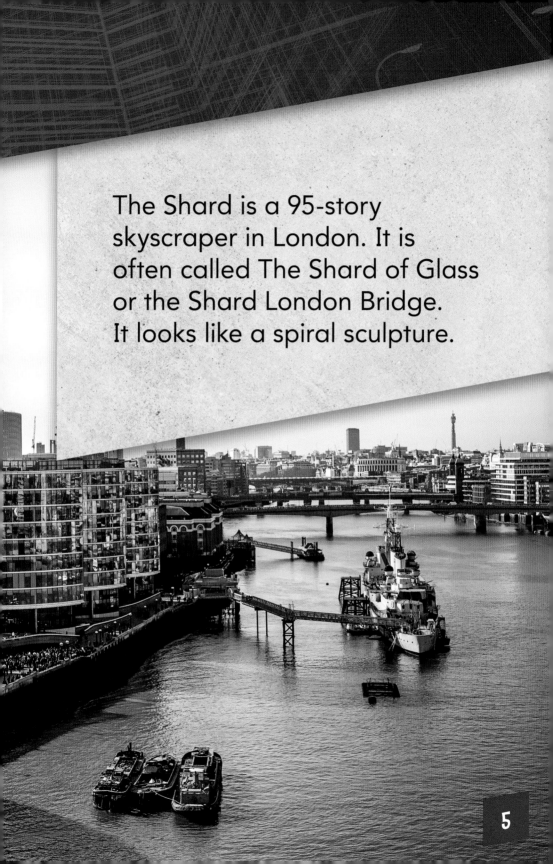

The Shard is a 95-story skyscraper in London. It is often called The Shard of Glass or the Shard London Bridge. It looks like a spiral sculpture.

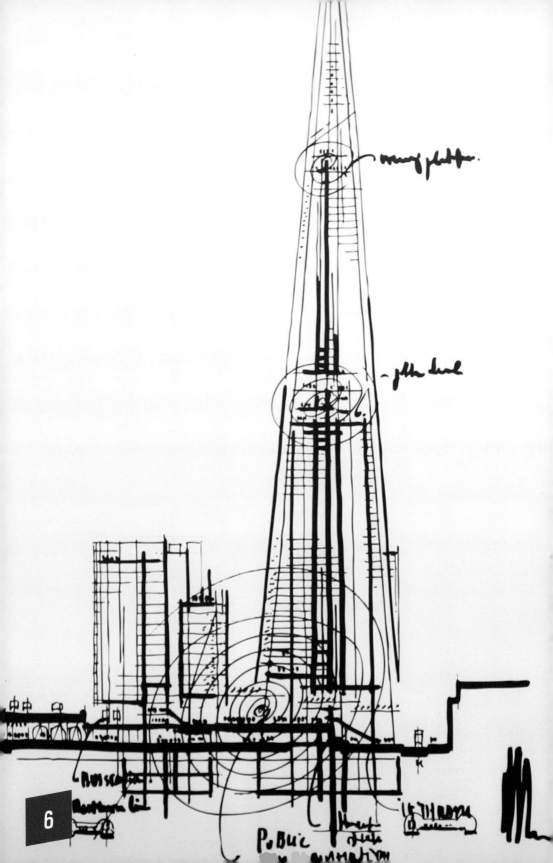

Irvine Sellars developed the Shard. He had a vision of a vertical city. He wanted it to be a place where people could live, work, and relax.

Renzo Piano was hired as the **architect**. He drew the design on a napkin in 2000. It was modeled after a shard of glass. It reflects **Neo-futurism** architecture.

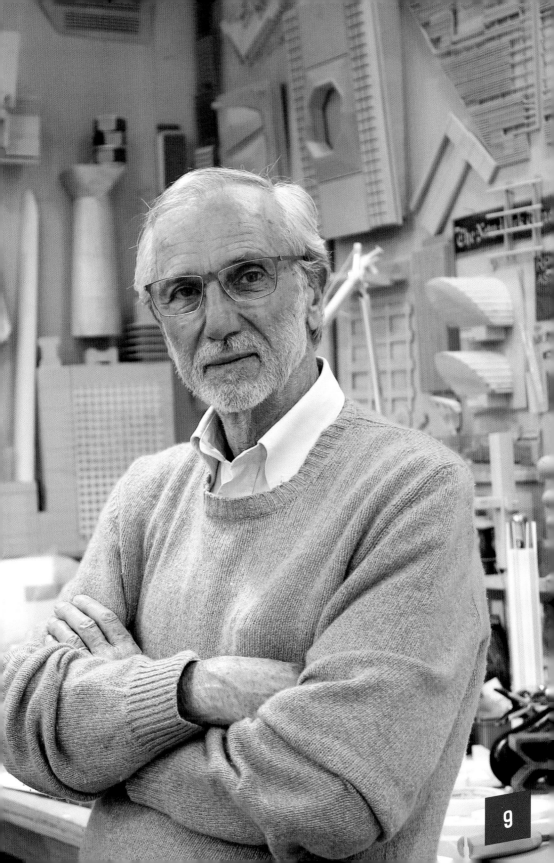

Building The Shard

Construction on The Shard started in March 2009. It took three years to complete. It opened in February 2013. It cost around $2.18 billion to build.

The Shard was built using concrete, steel, and glass. The concrete used to build The Shard could fill 22 Olympic-sized swimming pools! Around 95% of the materials used were recycled.

13

14

The Shard is 1,016 feet (310 m) tall. It is the tallest building in London.

16

The Shard has glass on all sides. There are 11,000 glass panels. The area of glass used is equal to eight football fields!

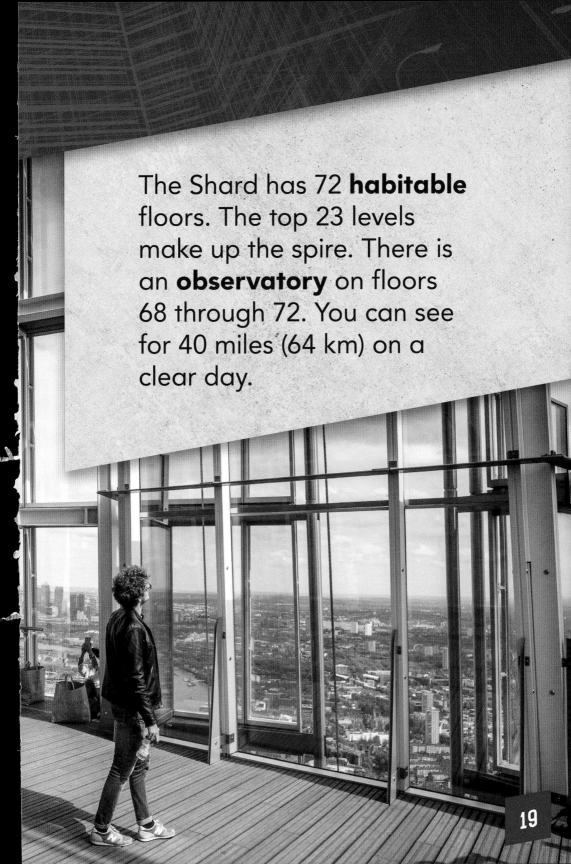

The Shard has 72 **habitable** floors. The top 23 levels make up the spire. There is an **observatory** on floors 68 through 72. You can see for 40 miles (64 km) on a clear day.

The Shard is home to many things. There are offices, shops, and restaurants. There is also a hotel and 10 **luxury** apartments.

magic 105·4

AT

THE VIEW
FROM THE SHARD

Keith
Hucksley –

Elizabeth
Moore –

30th January

More Facts

- The Shard has 44 elevators that travel 13 mph (70 kph). It takes less than one minute to get to the top.

- During construction a fox was found living on the 72nd floor. They believe it lived off food left behind by the workers. The workers named it Romeo.

- There is 200 miles (322 km) of wiring in The Shard. That is long enough to stretch from London to Paris!

Glossary

architect – a person who designs buildings and directs their construction.

habitable – capable of being lived in.

luxury – extremely nice.

Neo-futurism – a late 20th to early 21st century movement in the arts, design, and architecture.

observatory – a building that gives wide views.

Index

Online Resources

Booklinks
NONFICTION NETWORK
FREE! ONLINE NONFICTION RESOURCES

To learn more about The Shard, please visit
abdobooklinks.com. These links are routinely
monitored and updated to provide the most current
information available.